CONTENTS

Foreword

"I am about to do a new thing; now it springs forth, do you not perceive it? I will make a way in the wilderness and rivers in the desert."

–Isaiah 43:19

This study began from a desire to raise biblical literacy around women's stories in Scripture in fresh and relevant ways, as part of our ministry's focus on encouraging, equipping, and empowering women to embrace their gifts and callings and equipping congregations and communities to "build God's church together." Our guiding coalition, a cross-sector group of leaders from across the Reformed Church in America, came together in September 2019 to pray, vision, and innovate alongside our editor, the Rev. April Fiet. In true Holy Spirit fashion, a new thing sprang forth and we perceived it readily: a Bible study that embraced the "both/and" of our ministry, both #sheiscalled and #wearecalled. Things moved quickly after that. Dr. Travis West joined the effort as co-editor, and a diverse array of authors stepped up to contribute—theologians, pastors, professors, and the president of our historic seminary. Within a couple months' time, this first volume was ready for final editing and things were nicely on track for a print edition to be ready in time for Women in Ministry Sunday on May 17, 2020.

Then, in mid-March, the pandemic hit, and our world turned upside down. As our team grappled with an ever-changing landscape and traumatic circumstances in the early days of COVID-19, we wondered what would become of our project. How would we pivot to meet the new realities? As we prayed, God revealed it to us in real time and truly made a way in the wilderness of the pandemic for the She is Called Women of the Bible Study Series, Volume 1, to be produced as a PDF and shared digitally. The PDF was shared in plenty of time for Women in Ministry Sunday 2020 and just at a time when many leaders were wondering what to offer their communities as stay-at-home orders were extended, Eastertide was upon them, and Pentecost was on the horizon. The study fit perfectly into this season and was downloaded hundreds of times. By mid-June, the idea of a "master class" series developed. Over the summer, a virtual community of 150+ people gathered from all over North America to learn from the authors themselves and contemplate how these women's stories might inspire and impact their own. It was a time of great encouragement for so many and one of the blessings of the pandemic. From this Bible study, created to lift up the stories of our biblical mothers and sisters in the faith, emerged a community of God's beloved children who would never have had the chance to meet and share otherwise.

In these divisive, "either/or" times we are living in, how awesome that God provided us a space to do the "both/and" work of examining the gospel through the lens of women's stories. Historically, our understanding of the gospel has depended on the perspectives of men, who were typically focused on the stories of other men. And all of us, women and men, need to understand the stories of biblical women if we're going to understand the gospel itself, discover what it means to be called to embrace the gospel today, and live into what it means to be active parts of the body of Christ.

I am deeply grateful for those who worked on this study: our guiding coalition who imagined what it could be, our editors who labored over the content and concept with great care, and each of our authors, who readily jumped in to share their gift of the written word, crafting unique, engaging, historical, theological, and personal insights, and helping readers connect with practical application possibilities in #sheiscalled and #wearecalled sections. Their writing has been further enlivened by the stirring artwork of Crystal Wright and book design of Ben Snoek, whose creative gifts come together to make this print edition something inspiring and inviting for both women and men, people of different backgrounds and contexts, to explore as they seek to build God's church together.

Together in the Spirit's movement,

Rev. Liz Testa
Women's Transformation and Leadership
Reformed Church in America

Preface

    The stories we tell shape and transform us. They remind us of who we are and urge us to become the people we want to be. The Bible is full of stories, and when we gather together as a community, we retell these beloved stories to knit us together as a body, to remind us of who we are, and to inspire us to continue in our walks with Christ. One of the primary ways God chose to share with us was through stories. These stories reveal to us who God is and who God created us to be. They invite us to see our stories—our very lives—as part of God's unfolding story. Psalm 107 begins with these words, "Give thanks to the LORD, for he is good; his love endures forever. Let the redeemed of the LORD tell their story—those he redeemed from the hand of the foe" (NIV). As we read Scripture, we are telling our story, and we are opening ourselves to the possibility of being transformed as we tell it.

    We tell these stories for the first time to the very youngest in our midst, and we tell them again to those who have already heard them many times before. Sunday school classroom flannelgraphs and coloring pages bring these stories off the pages of the Bible so that children might experience them for themselves. In the story of Joseph, we see the power of forgiveness, and we see God's ever-present influence in our lives—even when we land in a pit or a dungeon. The story of David's bravery in the face of Goliath helps us imagine that sometimes the most unexpected is the one God chooses. The story of Saul's conversion and renaming on the road to Damascus teaches us that no one is too far outside God's movement to be embraced by it. We tell these stories again and again because, as Chuck DeGroat writes, "The Christian Story ... is a story of union and communion, of wholeness and holiness. It tells us who we are."[1] From our earliest years, these Bible stories teach us that God is involved in the lives of God's people. We tell these stories to Sunday school children and hear them preached and taught because we believe these stories can, by the power of the Spirit, transform us into the people of God.

We are also shaped by the stories we avoid telling. The Bible is filled with extraordinary stories of women that we often tuck away or overlook. The power of these stories might be uncovered or shared in small group Bible studies or in times of personal devotion, but in many places, these stories are never read or preached about. The Bible offers us the story of the prophet Miriam, who led a jubilant song of worship after God delivered them through the parted sea. In the house of Simon the Leper, a woman poured out an alabaster jar and anointed the head of Jesus, a priestly act that defied tradition and expectation. Martha, in the valley of grief in the loss of her brother, spoke words of great faith, "Even now I know that God will give you whatever you ask of him" (John 11:22). Through these stories of women in Scripture, God offers us the opportunity to experience transformation in our lives.

Some of these stories are difficult stories of pain and grief. They cause us to reevaluate our lives, to repent, and to strive onward to become the people we were created to be. As Brené Brown writes, "Owning our story can be hard but not nearly as difficult as spending our lives running from it. Embracing our vulnerabilities is risky but not nearly as dangerous as giving up on love and belonging and joy—the experiences that make us the most vulnerable. Only when we are brave enough to explore the darkness will we discover the infinite power

---

[1] Chuck DeGroat, *Wholeheartedness: Busyness, Exhaustion, and Healing the Divided Self* (Grand Rapids, MI: Eerdmans, 2016), 189.

of our light."[2] We read, tell, and engage with these stories not just because they are inspirational, but also because these stories invite us to experience God in ways that are sure to transform our lives.

The She Is Called Women of the Bible Study Series was created to help us dig deeply into the stories of biblical women so that we all might be challenged, strengthened, and encouraged in our faith. These stories are our stories, and they are "inspired by God and [useful] for teaching, for showing mistakes, for correcting, and for training character, so that the person who belongs to God can be equipped to do everything that is good" (2 Timothy 3:16-17, CEB). These stories are not easy stories—in fact, some of them are quite challenging—but they have been given to us by God as gifts. The authors of the studies in this book are able guides who can help us navigate these powerful stories. We are asked only to open these stories and read. Through the power of the Spirit, the gifts of these stories will become alive in our hearts and in our lives.

In this study, you will find nine sessions, each focused on a biblical woman or biblical pairing of people. Take time to read the key Scripture passages listed before reading the reflection provided by the author. These studies have been formatted with an opening prayer and discussion questions at the end to guide you, whether you are studying as an individual or as part of a group, and to help you explore these stories with fresh eyes, whether you have read them before or are reading them for the first time. It is our hope that this Women of the Bible study series will stretch and strengthen you as you read about and learn from these marvelous stories.

May God bless your reading and your studies through the power of the Spirit!

—Rev. April Fiet and Rev. Dr. Travis West

---

[2] Brené Brown, *The Gifts of Imperfection: Let Go of Who You Think You're Supposed to Be and Embrace Who You Are* (Center City, MN; Hazelden, 2010), 6.

Shining

PHOEBE

Phoebe: Deacon and Benefactor

By Dr. Rob Dixon

Prayer

As you start the study, invite the Lord to meet you, to open your heart to get to know a new Bible hero. In particular, ask God to inspire you through Phoebe's example of leadership and generosity.

Key Scripture

We find Phoebe's story recounted in just two Bible verses: Romans 16:1-2 (NIV):

"I commend to you our sister Phoebe, a deacon of the church in Cenchreae. I ask you to receive her in the Lord in a way worthy of his people and to give her any help she may need from you, for she has been the benefactor of many people, including me."

Main Point

In this study, we will meet another woman whose story has too often been obscured or minimized in the study of the first church. In the process, Phoebe will challenge us to become more effective leaders and benefactors to others.

👤 Introduction to Phoebe

What do we know about Phoebe, both from this short text and from the larger New Testament context?

First, Phoebe was part of a larger cohort of women who partnered closely with the Apostle Paul, women such as Chloe (1 Corinthians 1:11), Nympha (Colossians 4:15), Apphia (Philemon 2), Euodia and Syntyche (Philippians 4:2-3), and Junia (Romans 16:7). Sometimes Paul gets labeled as being "anti-women," but Phoebe and her sisters would surely testify otherwise.

Next, the text tells us that Phoebe's home base is Cenchreae, a coastal town about five miles southeast of the city of Corinth. From Paul's words in Romans 16, we know that there was a Christian church in Cenchreae, and that Phoebe had some sort of significant role in the life of the church at Cenchreae.

Third, the passage starts with Paul "commending" Phoebe to the Roman Christians, the letter's original recipients. Why would Paul feel the need to commend Phoebe to the Romans? One possible answer is that Phoebe carried the letter to Rome on Paul's behalf. Indeed, a number of theologians believe that not only was Phoebe the letter-carrier, she also likely explained the letter to its first hearers. As one scholar has noted, "Phoebe carried under the folds of her robe the whole future of Christian theology."[1]

📕 Digging Deeper

Beyond this introduction, these two verses offer some key details regarding Phoebe's life and vocation. First, Paul calls her a "deacon." The Greek word for "deacon" is *diakonos*, and it is elsewhere translated as "servant" or "minister." In his essay "What Can We Say About Phoebe?," Jeffrey Miller argues that Paul's usage of *diakonos* in Romans 12 carries with it the notion of leadership. He writes, "Phoebe's description as *diakonos* includes the qualifying phrase 'of

---

[1] Attributed to a theologian named Rénan and quoted in any number of theological reflections on the book of Romans.

the congregation in Cenchreae.' This localization of Phoebe's position strongly suggests Paul had in mind a specific status rather than general comportment."[2]

In other words, when Paul commends Phoebe to the Romans, he chooses to illuminate her specific leadership role within the Christian community in Cenchreae. Phoebe the deacon is a leader, and Paul wants the Romans to know it. Perhaps knowing her leadership credentials would make the Romans listen more closely as she unrolled the scroll to begin her reading of the letter.

Second, Paul refers to Phoebe as a "benefactor." In the Greco-Roman world, benefactors, or patrons, funded various social enterprises. As a benefactor, Phoebe was a woman of some means who was generous with her support of others, Paul in particular. Theologian Marg Mowczko writes, "As well as being an important part of Roman society at all levels, patronage was also important in the church. Edwin Judge has remarked, 'Christianity was a movement sponsored by local patrons to their social dependents.'"[3]

As a benefactor, Phoebe was a woman of some means who was generous with her support of others, Paul in particular.

What's the significance of Paul commending Phoebe to the Romans by noting her status as a benefactor? Perhaps it testified to her character. The Roman church should heartily welcome this generous, committed, and sacrificial woman into their community.

---

[2] Miller, Jeffrey D. "What Can We Say About Phoebe?" *CBE International*, Priscilla Papers, 2011, www.cbeinternational.org/resources/article/priscilla-papers/what-can-we-say-about-phoebe.

[3] Mowczko, Marg. "Wealthy Women in the First-Century Roman World and in the Church." Marg Mowczko, 30 Dec. 2019, margmowczko.com/wealthy-women-roman-world-and-church/.

#SheIsCalled and We Are Called

What is the message of these two verses for us today? How might Paul's words about Phoebe challenge us in the various contexts in which we find ourselves? The answer to these questions could well correlate to the two titles that Paul gives Phoebe in Romans 16:1-2.

First, she is a deacon. Part of her calling from God was to lead the church, God's people. If you are a woman, how are you leading in your church context? If you are a man, are you making space for women and girls to assume leadership roles in your church, your business, your home? If not, how can you follow Paul's example and champion the gifts and service of women in your context? How might you lose your life (Mark 8:34-38) in order to more fully bless the people of God?

Secondly, Phoebe was a "benefactor of many people," including Paul. There are plenty of broken and hurting people in our church communities. How might Jesus be inviting you to become a benefactor to those around you, and what could that look like tangibly for you?

Conclusion

In her biography of Phoebe, Paula Gooder notes that, in Greek, her name means "shining."[4] In our leading and in our generosity, may we always shine the light of Christ as Phoebe did.

🗨 Discussion Questions

1. Who has been a Phoebe in your life? In your congregation?
2. How does Phoebe's story encourage you in your own story of faith?
3. What surprised you in this Bible study session?
4. What do you hear the Spirit saying to you/your family/your church/your community?

---

[4] Paula Gooder, *Phoebe: A Story*, Downers Grove, IL: InterVarsity Press, 2018, 230.

Dr. Rob Dixon *lives in Clovis, California, with his wife, Amy, and four amazing kids. For the last 24 years, Rob has served as a campus minister with InterVarsity Christian Fellowship, and he graduated in 2018 from Fuller Theological Seminary with a doctorate degree focused on thriving ministry partnerships between women and men. Rob's personal mission statement is to challenge the people of God to embrace a theology and practice of gender equality. He is the author of the forthcoming book,* Together in Ministry: Women and Men in Flourishing Partnerships, *coming in summer 2021 from InterVarsity Press Academic.*

Notes

Come see

a man who told me EVERYTHING He cannot be the MESSIAH?

The Samaritan Woman at the Well

Called to Be a Disciple and Evangelist

By Rev. Dustyn Elizabeth Keepers

🕯 Prayer

God, you who met the Samaritan woman at the well that day, meet us in this story from Scripture and in our lives this day. Amen.

🔑 Key Scripture

"She said to the people, 'Come and see a man who has told me everything I've done! Could this man be the Christ?'"
—John 4:29, CEB

⭐ Main Point

The Samaritan woman whom Jesus meets at Jacob's Well gleans much from her long conversation with Jesus. When she discovers his identity as the Messiah she leaves her water jar, much like the disciples left their nets, and becomes an effective evangelist to her community.

👤 Introduction to the Samaritan Woman at the Well

Though we are not told this woman's name, she has the longest conversation with Jesus of any character in the book of John. Yet, throughout the years she has often been maligned or misunderstood because of her sexual history. This history often colors our reading of this episode, so before diving into the rest of her conversation with Jesus, let's look at this aspect more closely.

Certainly, five marriages is a high number. But in this time period, it was not unreasonable. Widowhood was a common experience in a culture where women were married very young. Divorce in order to gain a more socially advantageous marriage was also not uncommon, though it is unclear if the Samaritans allowed women to apply for it without a male guardian as the Romans may have. So, it seems most likely that her many marriages were not a result of her choice.[1]

Her current situation, living with a man who is not her husband, could be the result of several possible scenarios. She could be a concubine, which was a legal arrangement but with lesser status than marriage. If the two partners in the relationship were not of equal social status or wanted to avoid inheritance issues, they might choose this option. She could also be a second wife, a role which was also socially acceptable but not considered of the same status as the first wife. Perhaps most importantly, we should notice that Jesus does not condemn her status but simply acknowledges "what you have said is true" (4:18), as he continues to engage her in theological dialogue, to which we now turn.

📖 Digging Deeper

Jesus meets this Samaritan woman at Jacob's Well after a morning's journey and disregards social custom by asking her for a

---

[1] For a more detailed examination of the historical record on women and marriage in this time period and the Samaritan woman's story in particular see *Women in the World of the Earliest Christians* by Lynn Cohick (Baker Academic, 2009), 99-128.

drink. This boundary crossing between a Jew and a Samaritan sparks a conversation about their theological differences. Like all Samaritans, she traces her ancestry back to Jacob. She reveres this place but is curious about this stranger who promises something greater. She has a good grasp on her own tradition's beliefs, so she asks, "Are you greater than our father Jacob who gave us this well?" (4:12). And yet, she is eager for the eternal abundance Jesus promises.

Jesus promises living water that gives eternal life and invites her to bring the rest of her household—specifically, her husband—to receive the goodness he is offering. This turns the conversation to her personal history and current marital situation. She responds honestly and succinctly, "I have no husband" (4:17). And Jesus affirms that what she has said is true and indicates that he has seen and knows her more fully than she might have guessed. Without judgement, he relays the fuller story of her past, and she immediately understands that he is a prophet who knows and speaks the truth. She decides to take their theological discussion a step further and asks him about the proper place for worship, one of the major differences between Jews and Samaritans. In response, Jesus speaks of a future time when all true worshipers of God will worship not in a particular place but "in the Spirit and in truth" (4:23-24).

Jesus's mention of the future raises her hopes for the coming Messiah. She speaks of her anticipation of the fuller understanding she will receive when the Messiah comes. In response Jesus declares, "I am he." In a sudden turn, this woman from whom Jesus earlier asked for a drink, has now found her own thirst for theological understanding quenched. She has met the Messiah, the one she has been hoping for. At that moment, the disciples interrupt their conversation, but she has heard all she needs to hear. She drops her water jar and rushes back to the village and says to everyone she meets, "Come and see a man who told me everything I have ever done. He cannot be the Messiah, can he?" (4:29).

#SheIsCalled and We Are Called

The Samaritan woman listens with open attentiveness to Jesus as she asks him questions about her faith and hope. The longer she talks with him, the more her understanding grows until she sees the full truth: Jesus is the Messiah. Throughout this conversation she demonstrates a posture of discipleship, learning from Jesus, and now #SheIsCalled as an evangelist. She leaves her water jar behind—just as the disciples left their fishing nets—a sign of her complete embrace of this calling to follow Jesus. She returns to her town and effectively shares her own experience with Jesus, inviting the villagers to come and see if they reach the same conclusion about him. In the end, "Many Samaritans from that city believed in him because of the woman's testimony" (John 4:39, NRSV).

> *Our callings are opportunities to turn personal growth in faith into action for the sake of others.*

This woman without a name is a wonderful model for all of us on our own journey of faith. Her actions invite us to stay connected to Jesus and ask questions about our faith in order to come to a fuller understanding of it. She models a way of doing this with both conviction about what she has learned in the past and also openness to discovering new things about what God is doing in the world. But just as our growth in faith is not only for our own benefit, the Samaritan woman takes her new learning and is propelled into action around her calling. She reaches out to her community and invites them to join her on the journey. Whether we feel called to evangelize as she does or we are called to use our gifts in other ways, her story reminds us that our callings are opportunities to turn personal growth in faith into action for the sake of others. This is the movement of all disciples—growing in faith through relationship with Jesus and moving outward to use our gifts for the sake of the world.

Conclusion

Jesus does not judge this woman's history, though many Christian interpreters have. Instead, through her conversation with Jesus, we discover a model for discipleship that is open to discovering a fuller understanding of God's action in the world. Through her response to Jesus as an evangelist, we are reminded that being a follower of Jesus calls us to put our gifts into action for the sake of others.

💬 Discussion Questions

1. The nameless woman at the well was called to be a disciple and evangelist. What is God whispering to you about your own calling?
2. Who told you about Jesus? Who in your life witnessed to you that they knew and were known by Jesus?
3. What surprised you in this Bible study session?
4. What do you hear the Spirit saying to you/your family/your church/your community?

Rev. Dustyn Elizabeth Keepers *is a Ph.D. candidate in Systematic Theology at Wheaton College Graduate School. Her current research centers on John Calvin, ecclesiology, and feminist theology. Dustyn is also an ordained minister of Word and sacrament in the Reformed Church in America and previously served as a pastor at North Holland Reformed Church in Holland, Michigan.*

to

Embrace

& times to refrain from

embracing

3

A Time to Embrace and a Time to Refrain from Embracing!

By Rev. Denise L. Posie

♦ Prayer

Almighty God, you are our King, Redeemer, Savior, and Lord. We welcome the presence of your Holy Spirit to lead and guide us in all areas of life. Help us to live into our true selves and to align with what is in your heart. Help us to be sensitive to the pain and joy of other women and men who are working in your church. Teach us when to embrace and when to refrain from embracing. We desire your perfect will in all things and at all times. Help us to tell our own stories and to be a witness to others of your greatness, faithfulness, and love. In Jesus's mighty name, we pray. Amen.

⚷ Key Scripture

Books of Esther and Ecclesiastes
"For everything there is a season, and a time for every matter under heaven ... a time to embrace, and a time to refrain from embracing." —Ecclesiastes 3:1, 5

★ Main Point

A strong sense of identity is necessary for a woman [or man] to keep their balance in her [or his] calling and work ... it's about integrity, about staying true to this authentic personhood in the variety of life

situations. … Jesus himself was the epitome of a person with a strong sense of personhood.
—Mary Ellen Ashcroft[1]

It has been frequently pointed out that God makes no explicit appearances in the book of Esther. In light of this, Arie C. Leder states the following: "Wisdom categories have been employed to understand historical narratives in which God is not overtly active."[2] This Bible study brings the historical narrative of Esther into conversation with part of the wisdom tradition found in Ecclesiastes 3:1-8.

👤 Introduction to the Book of Esther

The reader sees surprising glimpses of wealth, royalty, power, beauty, rejection, and deception during the reign of King Ahasuerus[3] in the citadel of Susa in Persia. As the balance of power in the region shifted from Babylon to Persia, many Jews remained scattered throughout the 127 Persian provinces. The Jews are quiet and hidden until the presence of evil manifests through the king's highest official, Haman. One person brings about a significant shift in the narrative, showing human sinfulness and brokenness.

Major incidents occur inside and outside of the palace gates, all posing tension, chaos, and consequences.

We will explore two of those incidents in this Bible study. The first is when First Lady Queen Vashti, a Gentile, is presented with a command from the king to come to his banquet. The second incident occurs with First Lady Queen Esther, a Jew. Her cousin Mordecai stands on the outside of the gate. He commands her to go before the king to

---

[1]   Quoted in Ellen Banks Elwell and Joan Bartel Stough, *When There's Not Enough of Me to Go Around: Life Solutions to Perfectionism, People-Pleasing, and Performance Pressures* (Downers Grove, IL: InterVarsity Press, 2002), 48.

[2]   Arie C. Leder, "Historical Narrative and Wisdom. Towards preaching Esther 'for such a time as this," *Acta Theologica* 2011 31(2): 135-158, accessed February 1, 2020, http://dx.doi.org/10.4314/actat.v31i2.7.

[3]   NRSV, KJV, ESV, JPS, NASB, and other translations use this name. NIV uses Xerxes.

save her people. Each queen has a strong sense of identity and makes a decision about how to respond.

Through the stories of these two women in the book of Esther, #SheIsCalled women and men are encouraged to understand who we are and the times and circumstances in which we live.

📖 Digging Deeper: Queen Vashti
Suggested text to read: Esther 1.

How do you respond when suddenly you find yourself in a compromising situation? Someone in a position of power and influence presses you to engage in something that goes against your values, your identity, and what God has created you to do? How likely will the way you handle this situation be influenced by pleasing others or choosing what you think is best for you? How willing are you to accept the consequences of your decisions, right or wrong? In light of these questions, let's take a closer look at Queen Vashti's dilemma.

When King Ahasuerus's entourage of seven came to bring Queen Vashti to his "special banquet" wearing the royal crown to show off her beauty to a room filled with high spirited men, she refused. The narrative does not explain why she responded this way, but Queen Vashti made a choice *not* to succumb to the king's pleasures, *not* to be put on display as the king's trophy. She did the unthinkable by saying no, and she was willing to accept the consequences. Queen Vashti was on point. The king was up to no good.

Once Queen Vashti made up her mind, she was ready to deal with the consequences. She teaches us about the role of integrity and courage; integrity takes courage. Although the women at her banquet overhear the conversation between the eunuchs and Vashti, she stands alone. She speaks up, and she speaks for herself. She is not powerless against a powerful king. She knows what she will and will not do, even with the exertion of power. The timing is right. Her decision to refuse the king is considered wrong. Her act of protest has a widespread effect on "all the nobles and the peoples of all the provinces of King

Ahasuerus" (1:16). Queen Vashti chooses to refrain from embracing the king's demand. "Vashti is never again to enter the presence of King Ahasuerus" (1:19).

Out of fear, King Ahasuerus's advisers ironically made sure Queen Vashti's act of protest received kingdom-wide attention in every household, the crown's (futile?) attempt to keep the women in the kingdom in line, respecting their husbands.

📗 Digging Deeper: Queen Esther
Suggested text to read: Esther 4-5.

How might you think or feel if asked to give up a place of comfort for a season of uncertainty? What safety nets do we depend on instead of depending on God, our lifeline? How empowering is it to take a look backwards to see God's activity in your life before moving forward? At what point are we willing to give up our comfort for the good of others? In light of these questions, let's take a closer look at Queen Esther's dilemma.

While what might seem like a dark cloud is hanging over Vashti's head, Queen Esther finds herself in the spotlight after learning from her cousin-guardian Mordecai about the impending annihilation of her people, the Jews. Although Esther is the queen of a Gentile nation, she is a Jew by birth. *Hadassah*, Esther's Hebrew name, means "myrtle," like an evergreen; myrtle symbolizes peace, joy, generosity, and justice. Her Persian name, Esther, means "the star." Biblically speaking, God uses his stars.

Esther 4:13-14 (NIV) is where we see Mordecai making a subtle yet compelling connection to the Divine for Queen Esther: "Do not think that because you are in the king's house you alone of all the Jews will escape. For if you remain silent at this time, relief and deliverance for the Jews will arise from another place, but you and your father's family will perish. And who knows but that you have come to your royal position for such a time as this?" God is in this!

Mordecai's response falls heavy onto Queen Esther's shoulders. Up to this point, she has not revealed her ethnicity to the king. She is in a position to save her people. Queen Esther is no longer that powerless young woman brought to the king's harem. Hegai, who was in charge of the harem, prepared First Lady Queen Esther well. Persian customs and culture are no longer foreign to her.

In Esther 4:15-16 (NIV), Queen Esther calls for the Jews in Susa to fast for her, eating and drinking nothing for three days and nights. She says, "When this is done, I will go to the king, even though it is against the law. And if I perish, I perish." There are sighs and relief. It is time to embrace the moment!

Queen Esther strategically sets the stage for her own banquets. It came at the right time, with the right audience and under the right circumstances. She is intelligent, courageous, and patient. Psalm 141:9-10 says, "Keep me from the snares they have laid for me, from the traps set by evildoers. Let the wicked fall into their own nets, while I pass by in safety." Haman is exposed and put to death on the erected pole in his front yard, but the order to destroy the Jews still stands.

Esther pours out her heart by falling at the king's feet, weeping and pleading mercy on behalf of her people. Her act of desperation is not a selfish move on her part. Queen Esther's tears cease as she arises in response to King Ahasuerus lowering his scepter, granting her the audience she desires. Favor follows Esther from the moment she came to the royal palace. The king's edict made it possible for the Jews to protect themselves and to be safe in every city in the kingdom. Queen Esther's actions help change the fate of her people.

#SheIsCalled and We Are Called

In our society, there is a notion that women should be passive and allow men to do whatever they desire. Or, maybe, an attractive woman is not taken seriously as an intellectual or as a businesswoman, and she is told she got ahead on her looks alone. In times of chaos and complexity of life in America, many women hear statements like "Go home."[4]

---

[4] "John MacArthur Told Beth Moore To 'Go Home' For Having The Audacity To Preach The Gospel And Help People," *Relevant*, October 21, 2019. www.relevantmagazine.com/current/john-macarthur-told-beth-moore-to-go-home-for-having-the-audacity-to-preach-the-gospel-and-help-people.

Esther and Vashti were not passive pawns in the Persian Empire. They leveraged their power to do good for themselves and others with less influence. Recently, in the United Kingdom, Prince Harry and his American wife, Meghan Markle, desired to "step back" as senior members of the royal family, which came as a great shock to Queen Elizabeth II and the world. The couple's decision to relinquish this birthright will have a tremendous effect on their lifestyle and relations with the monarchy. Claims of racism against Meghan as well as Harry's childhood memories of the paparazzi chase that killed his mother, Princess Diana, were significant factors for refraining from embracing a lifestyle of royalty.[5]

Today, women are saying no, and some men are speaking up with them. Sometimes we have to give up something good in order to receive God's best for us.

When conversing with young, aspiring Christian leaders, they express a desire to hear the voices of women and men who have stories about God's assignments for "such a time as this" (4:14). They want to know how you honored your call and used your God-given gifts. Women in a male-dominated environment have usually experienced many challenges. They want to know what sustained you.

It is vital for women and men who support women in leadership to share these incredible stories. Sometimes it takes just one person to change the trajectory of our God stories. Who needs to hear your story? Is it time to be silent or time to speak?

As women called to lead, we must be women of integrity. We cannot allow individuals to lead us into situations in which we are not supposed to be. We must know who we are and live into it. May we long for making lifegiving and sacrificial decisions as we lead and serve in God's world.

---

[5] William Booth and Karla Adam, "Harry and Meghan aim to 'step back' as senior royals and split time between Britain and North America," *The Washington Post*, January 8, 2020, accessed February 14, 2020, https://www.washingtonpost.com/world/prince-harry-and-meghan-to-step-back-as-senior-royals-and-split-time-between-britain-and-north-america/2020/01/08/564f3e32-3249-11ea-971b-43bec3ff9860_story.html.

Conclusion

Faced with their unique circumstances and challenges as women called to lead, the stories of Queen Vashti and Queen Esther interact with our own stories. Faced with our unique platforms, situations, and challenges, we are inspired to discern our times to embrace and times to refrain from embracing.

Even in Jesus's ministry, there were times he embraced and times he refrained from embracing.

💬 Discussion Questions

1. In what ways do integrity, values, courage, and shame intersect in our stories?
2. Where are women, men, girls, and boys experiencing abuses of power—in your community, your church, your country, the world?
3. Where in your life might God be calling you to act "for such a time as this"?
4. What surprised you in this Bible study session?
5. What do you hear the Spirit saying to you/your family/your church/your community?

Rev. Denise L. Posie *has held several positions in the Christian Reformed Church in North America (CRCNA). She is currently the director of Leadership Diversity in the denominational office in Grand Rapids, Michigan. She serves as a Formation Group Leader at Calvin Theological Seminary and is passionate about developing leaders. She earned a Master of Divinity in Pastoral Leadership at Columbia International University in South Carolina. Denise moved to Kalamazoo, Michigan, in accepting a call to pastor at Immanuel Christian Reformed Church, where she served for 13 years.*

blessed

is she who

believed

Elizabeth and Mary: Called to Encourage One Another

By Rev. Dustyn Elizabeth Keepers

Prayer

Holy God, as we open your Word to study Elizabeth and Mary, open our eyes to see you, our ears to listen for you, and our hearts to perceive the ways you are at work in us and in the world. Amen.

Key Scripture

Luke 1:39-56
"And Mary said, 'My soul magnifies the Lord, and my spirit rejoices in God my Savior.'" —Luke 1:46-47

Main Point

When Mary and Elizabeth meet, the Spirit inspires them to more fully understand God's action in their own lives and in the world. Their encouragement and support for one another leads to some of the most beautiful words of praise to the Lord in Mary's Magnificat.

👤 Introduction to Elizabeth and Mary

In the opening chapter of Luke, not one, but two women of faith experience miraculous pregnancies. We meet Elizabeth first. She is the wife of Zechariah, a priest, and we are told "both of them were righteous before God, living blamelessly according to all the commandments and regulations of the Lord" (1:6). Yet, they had been unable to have a child until the Lord intervened.

Around the same time, unbeknownst to Elizabeth, her young relative Mary has also become pregnant through the Lord's intervention. The angel Gabriel announces to Mary that she has found favor with God and explains the Lord's plan for her and the son she will bear. When Mary is understandably astonished, the angel tells her about Elizabeth's unexpected pregnancy, presumably to reassure her or confirm the possibility of such a miracle. At this news, she answers, "I am the Lord's servant, may your word to me be fulfilled" (1:38). After the angel leaves, Mary immediately sets out to see Elizabeth.

📖 Digging Deeper

It is unclear how well Mary and Elizabeth knew one another before this meeting recorded in Luke 1:39-56. Presumably Mary lived near Nazareth, and Elizabeth lived near Jerusalem where her husband worked in the temple. But whether they are close or more distant relatives, their shared experience seems to quickly draw them together. Elizabeth instantly and prophetically knows what has happened to Mary. As soon as Mary greets her, she is filled with the Holy Spirit and exclaims, "Blessed are you among women and blessed is the child you will bear!" Elizabeth blesses Mary with the same blessing Deborah, the judge and prophet, once pronounced on the brave and bold Jael (Judges 5). Mary is blessed for believing the Lord's promises. In this way, Elizabeth's words anticipate Jesus's blessing of those who hear the word of the Lord and obey (Luke 11:28). She encourages Mary by celebrating her faith as well as her role as mother of Jesus.

In the same breath, Elizabeth speaks of the child still in Mary's womb as "Lord"—the Bible's first Christological confession! Before any of his miracles or teaching (or even seeing Jesus in the flesh), Elizabeth responds to the question he will later ask his disciples: "Who do you say that I am?" (Luke 9:20). She calls him "Lord," the same word she has just used to speak of God. In Elizabeth's womb, the one who will grow up to become John the Baptist leaps for joy as the Holy Spirit comes upon his mother, the first to point to Jesus's identity as the Lord, the God who saves.

Elizabeth's prophetic exclamation of the truth about Mary and her son seems to further encourage Mary who is preparing to be the "servant of the Lord" (1:38). Others who have held this honorary title include Moses, Joshua, Abraham, David, and many prophets, including Hannah.[1] And, in response to Elizabeth's words, Mary speaks in poetic verses (as so many prophets do), a song reminiscent of Hannah's prayer in 1 Samuel 2:1-10. We often refer to this song/prayer as "The Magnificat" because it begins with the words, "My soul magnifies the

Lord and my spirit rejoices in God my Savior" (Luke 1:46-47). In response to what the angel has told her and encouraged by Elizabeth's prophetic recognition of God's work in her life, Mary celebrates what God has done and will do "from generation to generation."

Can you imagine the energy and excitement in the room as these two women share this inspiring Spirit-filled moment together? The Lord is at work in each of their lives,

Sculpture of Mary and Elizabeth, Church of the Visitation, Ein Karem, Jerusalem, Israel.

---

[1] According to Jewish teaching, Hannah is considered one of the seven prophetesses of the Hebrew Bible (what many Christians refer to as the Old Testament).

and they name it out loud for each other, like sparks flying back and forth between them. "Blessed is she who has believed that the Lord would fulfill all his promises to her!" (1:45). These two women have faithfully believed and now they help one another recognize God's action in their lives through their shared experience of pregnancy. And in that moment of encouragement, the Spirit inspires them further to declare the Lordship of Christ and to celebrate God's good deeds to all God's people! These magnificent words echo through the generations to inspire and encourage us all.

#SheIsCalled and We Are Called

We often hear the various parts of this story in isolation from each other. Perhaps during Advent, we hear the Magnificat sung or read, or we're likely to hear the angel's announcement to Mary and her response, "I am the Lord's servant." Yet, it is important to remember that the Magnificat does not immediately follow from Mary's response to the angel. Rather, it comes after she runs to Elizabeth who, by the power of the Spirit, sees the significance of what is happening to Mary and celebrates her faithfulness in it. Elizabeth's prophetic role calls forth Mary's song of praise which itself echoes prophecies of old. In this brief episode, both of these women are called to speak God's truth, and when they do so, they encourage and inspire one another—and us besides.

Though of course we don't know all the details of their relationship, this story invites us to imagine Mary coming perhaps to offer her help and support during Elizabeth's pregnancy as well as to find reassurance of the truth of the angel's words to her. We can imagine Elizabeth taking on the role of a wise mentor who sees God at work in her young niece's life and names it. She reminds Mary that she is blessed, not just because she bears this child, but because she is a young woman of faithfulness. Mary receives this encouragement and is empowered to declare the word of the Lord with boldness and beauty, living into her calling as a "servant of the Lord."

How might we each be called to play both of these parts in our own relationships: helping and supporting one another, identifying

God's work in the lives of others, encouraging one another and allowing the encouragement of others to inspire boldness in our own faith?

Conclusion

Though Mary declares herself the Lord's servant after the angel announces Jesus's birth to her, the prophetic words of her relative Elizabeth seem to further confirm this miracle to her and inspire her to celebrate it. Following Elizabeth's declaration of the Lord's work in her life as a blessing, Mary responds: "My soul magnifies the Lord and my spirit rejoices in God my Savior…" This story reminds us that encouragement is a Spirit-inspired gift we can offer others. And it prompts us to contemplate how our encouragement of others might bring praise to the Lord.

💬 Discussion Questions

1. Who in your life can you encourage or empower in their service to the Lord by naming their gifts and contributions to the kingdom?
2. Who in your life can you seek support, guidance, and encouragement from as you explore your place in the world?
3. What surprised you in this Bible study session?
4. What do you hear the Spirit saying to you/your family/your church/your community?

Rev. Dustyn Elizabeth Keepers *is a Ph.D. candidate in Systematic Theology at Wheaton College Graduate School. Her current research centers on John Calvin, ecclesiology, and feminist theology. Dustyn is also an ordained minister of Word and sacrament in the Reformed Church in America and previously served as a pastor at North Holland Reformed Church in Holland, Michigan.*

Co-workers

IN

Christ

Jesus

5

Priscilla and Aquila: The First Century's Dynamic Duo

By Rev. Tim Breen

🔥 Prayer

Triune God, Jesus prayed that we would be one—in him and as a body. As we study the team ministry of Priscilla and Aquila, unite us in purpose as we seek to show your love to the world. Amen.

🔑 Key Scripture

Acts 18:1-4, 24-26
"Greet Prisca and Aquila, who work with me in Christ Jesus."
—Romans 16:3

⭐ Main Point

Priscilla and Aquila, friends of Paul and mentors to Apollos, demonstrate the daring and beautiful possibilities of men and women working together for the flourishing of the kingdom.

👤 Introduction to Priscilla and Aquila

History and fiction are replete with stories of dynamic duos. Cleopatra and Mark Antony. Romeo and Juliet. Sonny and Cher. Mr. Incredible and Elastigirl. These powerful pairs united their individual gifts and abilities to accomplish incredible things.

The Bible also records important husband-and-wife combinations. Abraham and Sarah. Moses and Zipporah. Ruth and Boaz.

But no marriage was quite like that of Priscilla and Aquila. And consequently, no ministry was quite like theirs. Crazy as it sounds, Scripture suggests that without Priscilla and Aquila, *the church might not have turned out the way that it did.*

Priscilla and Aquila were tentmakers native to Rome. After the persecution of the Jewish people under the Emperor Claudius, they made their way to Greece, where they encountered the Apostle Paul and tutored the dynamic evangelist Apollos. Their impact on these Christian leaders – and the bravery they demonstrated within the early church—became legendary, and Priscilla and Aquila are referenced in four different New Testament books.

📙 Digging Deeper

Priscilla and Aquila are a fascinating study in men and women working together for the good of the church and the cause of the kingdom.

In certain biblical references, Priscilla is called by the more formal name "Prisca." That the writers felt comfortable at other points to use her nickname (think Robert/Bobby) suggests to me that Priscilla is a warm-hearted, gracious woman who doesn't take herself too seriously. So I'll continue to refer to her by that name. (Secondary motivation: "Priscilla and Aquila" sound like a fantastic couple from a Dr. Seuss book: *Priscilla and Aquila and their vanilla gorilla like to drink sarsaparilla on their way to Manila.* Sorry, I'll stop.)

But what's even more interesting about the references to this couple is the order in which their names are mentioned. In the seven references to this couple, the wife is mentioned before the husband five times. This is somewhat uncharacteristic of the naming conventions in the Bible and suggests that Priscilla played a leading role in their ministry work.

Priscilla and her husband appear first in Acts 18. They have come to the Greek city of Corinth as refugees from the racist purge of Rome by the Emperor Claudius. But this anti-Semitic terror did not quash their spirit, and the couple resourcefully set up a tentmaking shop in Greece.

It was there that they first encountered the Apostle Paul. Paul would later note that he came to Corinth "in weakness, fear, and trembling" (1 Corinthians 2:3). But Priscilla and Aquila welcomed him into their workplace, providing him with meaningful employment that facilitated his missionary activities.

After "some time" in Corinth, Paul determined to return to Syria. Priscilla and Aquila, committed to the early Christian ministry, accompanied Paul across the Aegean Sea to Ephesus, where their ministry continued. Acts 18:24 notes that it was in Ephesus that they met the Egyptian evangelist named Apollos. While Apollos was "a learned man" who spoke "accurately" and "with great fervor," his knowledge of the way of God was incomplete (18:24). Recognizing the opportunity to invest in this young leader, Priscilla and Aquila invited him into their home and provided deeper instruction.

Acts' narrative on Priscilla and her husband goes dark after this, but there is good indication that the couple remained active in their support of the early church. In his catalog of greetings to the Roman church (Romans 16), Paul sends his regards to Priscilla and Aquila. Some time after they had been expelled from the capital city, it appears they have returned!

As if this wasn't courageous enough, Paul notes that Priscilla and Aquila "risked their necks for me" (16:3). Bishop Handley Moule translates this passage, "For my life's sake Priscilla and Aquila submitted their own throats to the knife."

We don't know what this great act of bravery was, but it was sufficient to have impacted Paul long after the fact. Did they smuggle him out? Did they publicly defend him? Did they borrow a great deal of money to facilitate his work? The details are unclear, but the importance was not.

> *The details are unclear, but the importance was not.*

Priscilla and Aquila make two more appearances in the New Testament: 1 Corinthians 16:19, where they are with Paul, and again in 2 Timothy 4:19, where the author's last testament is not complete without a final word of loving correspondence with the couple, who have evidently returned to Ephesus.

#SheIsCalled and We Are Called

The story of Priscilla and Aquila holds out a cache of important truths. At the surface, it demonstrates the added value of men and women partnering over the long term for the cause of Christ.

But there are more specific elements that intersect with our realities. First, it is clear from their wide travels that Priscilla and Aquila recognized their citizenship was in heaven (Philippians 3:20). They were at home in Rome, Corinth, Ephesus, and anywhere else that their mission called them. Their work calls to mind the second-century *Epistle to Diognetus*, where it is said of Christians,

> They live in their own countries, but only as nonresidents; they participate in everything as citizens, and endure everything as foreigners. Every foreign country is their fatherland, and every fatherland is foreign.[1]

In our increasingly transient society—and in an era with ongoing cultural change—it remains essential to keep our spiritual bearings. We are members of Christ and citizens of his kingdom first.

---

[1] Peter Kriby, "Epistle to Diognetus" 5:5, trans. by J. B. Lightfoot, EarlyChristianWritings.com, http://www.earlychristianwritings.com/text/diognetus-lightfoot.html, accessed February 14, 2020.

Secondly, Priscilla and Aquila's lives point out the importance of true Christian hospitality. When Paul arrived in their community, they gathered in a worn-out traveler. They provided shelter, company, and income for him, advancing his missionary ventures. In Ephesus, they followed the same template with Apollos, perhaps sharing what they had learned from Paul to strengthen the witness of this remarkable young preacher. Their table and living room became sources of encouragement and instruction for those who would teach the church at large. To what extent do we see our hospitality as a means of kingdom growth?

Lastly, Priscilla and Aquila's story is one of risk and obedience. Again, we are unclear about the details of their courageous act on Paul's behalf, but we know that it was a meaningful and potentially costly deed. When the moment arose, Priscilla and Aquila were willing to bear their throats to the blade for the sake of their friend and the cause of Christ.

Priscilla and Aquila are therefore great models for all men and women called to acts of courage. Adversities, inequities, and enemies will inevitably appear, and brothers and sisters in Jesus cannot recoil in the tough times. Like Priscilla and Aquila, they must be prepared to risk greatly for the ultimate good.

Conclusion

In Romans 16:3, Paul says "Not only I, but all of the churches of the Gentiles are grateful for [Priscilla and Aquila]." Their lives were testimonies of God's faithfulness to the refugee, the worker, the obedient, and the wise. And around the Mediterranean, their work was recognized.

Perhaps "all the churches of the Gentiles" should be expanded to include the churches of London, Shanghai, and New York. Perhaps all of us owe a debt to the earnest work of Priscilla and Aquila.

I just wonder if, whenever he sat down to write 2 Corinthians, Paul might also have been thinking about Priscilla and Aquila. Perhaps he was reflecting on the good old days around the tentmaking table.

Maybe in the sewing, the cutting, the praying and the planning, he found a bit of perspective on his life:

> For we know that if the earthly tent we live in is destroyed, we have a building from God, an eternal house in heaven, not built by human hands. For while we are in this tent, we groan and are burdened, because we do not wish to be unclothed but to be clothed instead with our heavenly dwelling, so that what is mortal may be swallowed up by life.
> —2 Corinthians 5:3-4

See, when you are a tentmaker, always patching holes, always repairing tears, always setting up and taking down, you long for something more. You long to see people in crisis be rescued. Your heart burns for the next generation of believers. You look to a heavenly home and know that your life is always in Christ. You can see that someday, what you have stitched and sewn, where you have invested, and the stakes you have sunk—as fleeting as they seem now—will matter forever.

And that is worth giving whatever it takes.

🗨 Discussion Questions

1. Who in your life do you sense God inviting you to offer hospitality to? How can your table and living room be sources of encouragement and support to weary travelers?
2. Where in your life could you live more courageously?
3. What surprised you in this Bible study session?
4. What do you hear the Spirit saying to you/your family/your church/your community?

 **Rev. Tim Breen** *is the lead pastor of the First Reformed Church in Orange City, Iowa. He has served as a member of the Women's Transformation and Leadership Guiding Coalition, and he blogs at www.telosblog.com.*

Notes

REMIND us who we are

6

Zipporah: Called to Remind Us Who We Are

By Rev. Dr. Denise Kingdom Grier

🕯 Prayer

Great I Am, light the path before us we pray. Remind us in you who we truly are and remind your church of the same. Amen.

🔑 Key Scripture

"On the way, at a place where they spent the night, the Lord met him and tried to kill him. But Zipporah took a flint and cut off her son's foreskin, and touched Moses' feet with it, and said, 'Truly you are a bridegroom of blood to me!' So he let him alone. It was then she said, 'A bridegroom of blood by circumcision.'"
—Exodus 24:26

⭐ Main Point

Flesh and blood have always been faithful reminders of God's covenant promises.

👤 Introduction to Zipporah

Zipporah the Midianite was a descendant of Midian, Abraham's son by his third wife Keturah. In Hebrew, her name means "bird" or "little bird." We first meet Zipporah—who later became Moses's wife—at a well in her hometown of Midian. At the well, she met Moses, who was fleeing from Egypt and from Pharaoh's judgment after he murdered an Egyptian (Exodus 2:15-22).

Zipporah and her six sisters were attending to their daily chores of drawing water and watering their father's flock. Moses was seated at the well nearby, no doubt dressed, painted, and speaking like an Egyptian dignitary. When local shepherds drove the sisters away from the well in an act of gender-based violence, Moses rose to their defense and he watered their father's flocks. Upon returning to the home of their father, the sisters reported the incident of the "Egyptian" stranger who had come to their aid. In gratitude, the father urged them to go back and bring the kind "Egyptian" Moses to their village, and soon after, Zipporah would become Moses's wife.

Zipporah only appears three times in Scripture: the first time at the well (Exodus 2), the second time while on the journey to Egypt (Exodus 4), and finally in the wilderness when Moses met her father Jethro who was accompanied by Zipporah and her sons (Exodus 18). Of her three appearances in the text, she only speaks one time, in Exodus 4. Ultimately, Zipporah is replaced by Moses's second wife, a Cushite woman.

📖 Digging Deeper

The long donkey ride on the way to Egypt left Zipporah, Moses, and their two children wanting for a good night's rest. During the night, God's hand of death came against Moses and "tried to kill him" (Exodus 4:24).

Wait. What? God had just given Moses an assignment to return to Egypt and demand that Pharaoh free the Hebrews from bondage. What's more, God had just revealed himself to Moses and demonstrated great power in and through him. Why would God want to kill Moses?

Whatever the reason, Zipporah had to think and act quickly in order to save her husband's life. Her response to her husband's impending death is to perform a circumcision on her son and toss the foreskin at her husband Moses. In order to understand this scene, some background information is in order.

Let's go back.

When Zipporah and her sisters spotted Moses the first time, they thought he was an Egyptian, and in many ways they were right. Moses had been in the household of Pharaoh in Egypt since infancy. His mannerisms and customs were shaped by his Egyptian upbringing. In fact, he most likely dreamt in the language of Pharaoh. Everything about him was Egyptian, except for one thing. Unlike his Egyptian peers, he was circumcised. Circumcision was not the same medical practice it is today, but circumcision was a sign of the covenant God had made with Abraham and his descendants. Zipporah had borne two sons to Moses, but he had failed to perform circumcision on his sons. Egypt had caused Moses to forget his roots—his identity—as a descendant of Abraham. Alas, he had forgotten his blood!

When Zipporah saw her husband dying before her eyes at the hand of the Lord, she made a split second decision to circumcise her son and throw his foreskin at the feet of her husband. This has to be the bloodiest scene in the book of Exodus since the massacre of Hebrew male children in chapter 1. It would be rivaled soon after as the blood of the Egyptian children ran cold at the final plague,

> *Egypt had caused Moses to forget his roots. Alas, he had forgotten his blood!*

as the blood of lambs was smeared on the doorposts of the Hebrew households that first Passover, and with the bloodying of the sea as the waters closed over the Egyptian army.

"You are a bridegroom of blood," Zipporah declares as she tosses flesh at Moses's feet. With the prowess of *The Lion King*'s Mufasa to his son, Simba, Zipporah's actions roar, "Remember who you are." *You, Moses, are of the bloodline of Abraham. As such, you should have circumcised your son soon after his birth. Remember who you are; you are a bridegroom of blood.* The trappings of Pharaoh's house made it easy for Moses to forget Abel's sacrifice, the ram who saved Isaac, and the Hebrew blood that ran through his veins. These people he was going to save were his own people, God's chosen people by blood.

In order to complete his assignment, Moses had to die. At least, the Egyptian in him had to die in order for the "bloody," Israelite Moses, in his truest identity, to fulfill the purpose for which he was born. Through Zipporah's quick-thinking actions, she evoked the covenant by demonstration so Moses would remember his roots. If he was going to Egypt to free his people, his identification with Egypt had to die. The flesh and blood in the hands of his wife Zipporah would not let Moses forget.

#SheIsCalled and We Are Called

The church is married to a bridegroom of blood. Christmas warns us that flesh and blood matter to God. Holy Week drags us reluctantly down the bloody path to Golgotha. Maundy Thursday leads us to a bloody table and to a garden where Judas Iscariot has blood on his hands. Blood and water flow from the side of the bridegroom in those last moments on the cross. After the resurrection, Jesus invited Thomas to touch him in the bloody parts, his hand and his side. We who are in Christ cannot deny the sacrifice, the pain, the very life that runs through our souls in the blood of Christ, our resurrected Lord.

We must remember who we are—bride of Christ, circumcised in our hearts, dead to sin, our flesh perpetually cast at the feet of Jesus in confession and repentance. That's who we are: dead because of our sins and alive because of Christ, through his life and by his blood.

Zipporah reaches across centuries to point to the Lord's table, the flesh and blood of the new covenant. Every time we gather for communion, her words should be told alongside Moses's, "Yes, Jesus, you are a Bridegroom of blood."

At first glance, the relationship between Zipporah and Moses looks like the familiar boy-rescues-girl tale. Zipporah and her sisters appear too weak to defend themselves from the threat of local shepherds at the well. And, here comes Moses to the rescue. Naturally, this man who rescued these vulnerable young women was a likely suitor for one of the daughters of the Priest of Midian, and they lived happily ever after.

Alas, this is no patriarchal fairy tale, and Zipporah is no damsel in distress. Where once she was the beneficiary of male benevolence, she then stepped in to save the life of the patriarch. Zipporah's story should always be told alongside Moses's, for without her, he would surely have died before returning to Egypt, still unclear about his true identity.

Conclusion

There are things in the culture, in society, and in this world that naturally attach themselves to us and disguise our true identity. Sometimes it's our careers, our family name, or our traditions that are such a part of us that we forget Paul's reminder that "our citizenship is in heaven" (Philippians 3:20), and our identity is hidden in Christ.

As we reflect on Zipporah's witness, let us consider this:

The Hebrew word for "remember" invites us to focus on a thing until it leads us to repentance. Ask God to help you remember the places and things in your life that you have attached to your identity. How might these things have been allowed to trump your identity in Christ? Ask God to reveal these places and/or things. Confess and repent.

Zipporah urges us to remember who we are in Christ. We are urged to die to all our false identities and to remember our true identity as siblings of the flesh and blood of the Bridegroom.

💬 Discussion Questions

1. In what ways do you see the church dying, as Moses was dying on that road to Egypt? What action can you take to remind the church of her true identity?
2. Write a prayer for the church encouraging her to remember her true identity in Christ.
3. What surprised you in this Bible study session?
4. What do you hear the Spirit saying to you/your family/your church/your community?

Rev. Dr. Denise Kingdom Grier *is lead pastor of Maple Avenue Ministries, a multi-ethnic, multicultural, and multi-generational congregation of the Christian Reformed Church and Reformed Church in America in Holland, Michigan. Dr. Grier's doctoral research interrogates a system of apartheid in the American church in order to redirect outreach practices toward what she calls Embracing, a reciprocal model of community engagement. She recently encapsulated her work and interests in the 1cor13project.com. Denise also serves as an RCA Global Mission partner with Setshabelo Family and Child Services, a nongovernmental organization that provides loving families for orphaned and vulnerable children in South Africa.*

Notes

7

Deborah: Embracing the Call of God

By Pastor Pam Otten

⚫ Prayer

I thank you, Lord, that you love to do extraordinary things through ordinary people like me. Release me from any limitations I, others, or the enemy have put on my life that have kept me from the great plans you have for me, so that I might wake up and arise to shine the glory of the Lord! Amen.

🔍 Key Scripture

"In the days of Shamgar son of Anath, in the days of Jael, the highways were abandoned; travelers took to winding paths. Villagers in Israel would not fight; they held back until I, Deborah, arose, until I arose, a mother in Israel. ... 'Wake up, wake up, Deborah! Wake up, wake up, break out in song! Arise, Barak! Take captive your captives, son of Abinoam.'"
—Judges 5:6–7, 12, NIV

⭐ Main Point

The Lord calls ordinary people to do extraordinary things that can only be accomplished through the Spirit.

👤 Introduction to Deborah

The story of Deborah in Judges 4 and 5 begins like many of the stories in the Book of Judges—the Israelites sinned against the Lord, and he turned them over to King Jabin of Canaan. This went on for 20 years until the Israelites cried out to the Lord for help. At that time, Deborah was leading Israel as a judge. She sent for Barak, a commander in Israel's army, and told him to go and fight Jabin's army led by Sisera.

Barak said he would only go if Deborah went with him. Deborah agreed but told Barak the honor will not go to him, because the Lord will deliver Sisera into the hands of a woman. When Barak's army advances, the Lord routes Sisera's army, and Sisera flees on foot. Sisera goes to the tent of Jael, the wife of Heber, because there was an alliance between King Jabin and Heber's family.

Jael invited Sisera in and served him refreshments. Sisera was so exhausted, he fell asleep. Jael took a hammer and pounded a tent peg into Sisera's temple, killing him. The Israelites fought against King Jabin until they destroyed him. Deborah and Barak sang a song of praise, and Israel had peace for 40 years.

📖 Digging Deeper

Deborah was a busy woman. Judges 4:5 says, "She held court under the Palm of Deborah between Ramah and Bethel in the hill country of Ephraim, and the Israelites went up to her to have their disputes decided." Deborah was a woman of great wisdom, revelation, and discernment. She also had a prophetic gift, including knowing the times and seasons of the Lord. She clearly heard the voice of the Lord.

Yet Judges 5:12 says, "Wake up, wake up, Deborah! Wake up, wake up, break out in song! Arise, Barak! Take captive your captives, son of Abinoam." Deborah and Barak needed to "wake up and arise" to a new revelation and dimension of their callings. The Lord was telling them to be alert and pay attention, as he was about to move in an extraordinary way.

Judges 5:7 says, "Villagers in Israel would not fight; they held back until I, Deborah, arose, until I arose, a mother in Israel." Of all the things Deborah could have legitimately called herself—judge, prophetess, deliverer, intercessor, worshiper—she chose to call herself a mother. She was first and foremost a mother. This much seems clear. But it is unclear who her children were: she was a mother "in Israel," but also a mother "over Israel" (it can be translated both ways). She saw all of Israel as her children and longed for *all* of her children (literal and figurative) to experience peace and security.

Notice the verse says no one in Israel would fight until Deborah "arose." The Israelites were beaten down by 20 years of slavery. They were too tired and discouraged to fight. They needed someone to inspire them, and the Lord chose Deborah. If she had not been obedient to act on what the Lord told her to do, nothing would have changed. She used the place of trust and authority she had been given as a judge to inspire Barak to raise up an army.

> *Deborah was a worshiping warrior.*

Deborah was a worshiping warrior. She found encouragement and strength in worship to be obedient to everything the Lord was asking her to do. If Deborah had played small in her life, she would not have had all the experiences that led to her being used by the Lord to deliver Israel from bondage. She would not have had wisdom and revelation to judge disputes. She would not have heard the Lord's strategic battle plans as an intercessor. She would not have extended her compassionate mother's heart beyond her family to all of Israel. She would not have brought healing and empowerment to a whole nation.

Barak was told to "arise and take captive your captives" (5:12). He was reluctant to go to war without Deborah, but in the end, he was obedient to raise up an army and go where Deborah commanded him. This step of obedience was also necessary to fulfill the plans of the Lord.

Deborah's story would not be complete without acknowledging Jael, another woman who stepped up to literally stake her claim in history. Jael was in the right place at the right time and did what she knew she had to do. Deborah called Jael "most blessed of tent-dwelling women" (5:24). Jael was a homemaker who was invaluable to winning the war.

#SheIsCalled and We Are Called

One of the most fun and exciting opportunities I have received in my life began because I was a mother. Twelve years ago, I was invited to join a group of women who were coming together for a radio station to fill each week with 24/7 women radio hosts. I was invited as a financial advisor, and since many of the show topics revolved around being a mother, my tagline became "The Financial Mom." I did a weekly radio show for five years, and I learned to talk for about fifty minutes of my hour time slot every week.

The Lord never wastes an experience, and I now realize this was the very beginning of my preaching training. My financial advice always came from a biblical perspective, and by the end of those five years, I knew I was preaching to an audience of thousands every week. Ultimately, this experience helped give me the courage to step out and start my own business. Looking back at my life so far, I see the Lord's hand in so many of my experiences, preparing me for what I am today: a co-vocational business owner and pastor of a church plant.

Let me encourage you. So often we are afraid to step out of our comfort zones and become everything the Lord has called us to be. It's a blessing the Lord doesn't give us the whole plan for our lives in advance, because most of us would answer with a resounding "No!" Don't let the enemy get in your head and tell you God will never use you to do great things. Don't let your fear of what others may think get in the way of being obedient to God and used to do extraordinary things.

The Lord prepared Deborah in the secret place of her worship, which helped her grow in confidence in hearing God's voice. Her intentional connection to God through worship gave her confidence as she discerned the time to go to war. The Lord will do the same with us. As we go deeper in relationship with God, God will guide us to clarity around our call for this season of kingdom work. God can use many ways to confirm it to us over and over. As Christ followers, we are embarking on an exciting journey of serving the Lord here on earth.

Conclusion

Women and men of God, it's time for you to be bold and courageous and do the unique and amazing things God is calling you to do. Wherever the Lord has placed you, will you accept the challenge to be a light in the darkness for the Kingdom of God? Will you encourage others to do it, too? Wake up and rise to shine the glory of God everywhere you go! You carry the hope this world needs—the hope of Jesus Christ—and it's time to stop hiding and playing small. A dying, hopeless world is waiting for you to be obedient. Believe and trust God has the very best plan for you, and follow him to where he is working today.

(For a deeper dive into the life of Deborah, read *The Deborah Anointing* by Michelle McClain-Walters.)

💬 Discussion Questions

1. What kinds of prayer practices have been helpful as you seek to draw closer to God?
2. Describe a time when God helped make clear something you were called to do.
3. What surprised you in this Bible study session?
4. What do you hear the Spirit saying to you/your family/your church/your community?

Pastor Pam Otten *is the pastor of Renew Church, a mobile church plant serving in low income housing in Sheboygan, Wisconsin. Pam's personal calling is to set people free from whatever holds them back from living an abundant life in Christ, through prophecy and healing prayer. She is a member of the Women's Transformation and Leadership Guiding Coalition.*

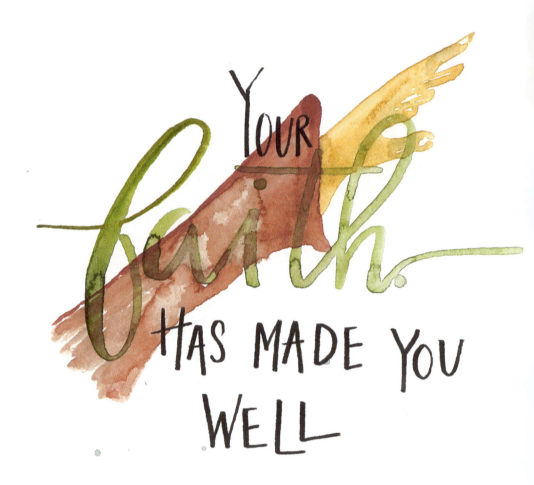

Your faith

HAS MADE YOU

WELL

8

"Daughter, Your Faith Has Made You Well."

By Rev. Alisha Riepma

Prayer

God, Son, and Holy Spirit, meet us in this space, whatever space we find ourselves in. Trinity, help us to learn more about who you are through this woman. Help us to see your image in the image bearer we find in this story. Help us to sympathize, grow, and lean into her story. Give us wisdom and gentleness with ourselves today. In your name we pray, amen.

Key Scripture

"Now there was a woman who had been suffering from hemorrhages for twelve years; and though she had spent all she had on physicians, no one could cure her. She came up behind Jesus and touched the fringe of his clothes, and immediately her hemorrhage stopped. Then Jesus asked, 'Who touched me?' When all denied it, Peter said, 'Master, the crowds surround you and press in on you.' But Jesus said, 'Someone touched me; for I noticed that power had gone out from me.' When the woman saw that she could not remain hidden, she came trembling; and falling down before him, she declared in the presence of all the people why she

*had touched him, and how she had been immediately healed. He
said to her, 'Daughter, your faith has made you well; go in peace.'"*
—Luke 8:43–48, NRSV

★ Main Point

When we feel outcast or in need of healing, cry out to Jesus. He
meets us where we are and reminds us of our belovedness.

👤 Introduction to the Woman with the Issue of Blood

The unnamed woman in this Gospel story is a woman who has
suffered for 12 years from a certain kind of bleeding; it is often translated
as "hemorrhaging." She has visited many doctors and healers, and none
of them has been able to heal her. It seems frenetic and like she is acting
out in a last ditch effort. Her very presence in a large crowd would be
frowned upon in this society because she is considered "unclean." Her
normal existence would often have been spent watching people skirt
around her to avoid the possibility of contact. No brushing or touching
or sharing friendly gestures on the path. She lived in isolation and would
have been known for her uncleanliness.

📖 Digging Deeper

To give a little background and context, this story of the woman
with the issue of blood is found in three of the gospel texts. For a
different angle to this story, let's detour to Mark's gospel. In the Gospel
of Mark, the writer gives us a richer understanding of Jesus's capacity
to love by using a particular literary method and another precious
story of healing. The method is what some scholars affectionately call
a "Markan Sandwich." The structure is: A1 - B - A2. The larger story
begins ("A1") with Jesus being abruptly greeted by a synagogue leader,
Jairus, who falls at Jesus's feet imploring him to heal his little daughter
who is at the point of death. In the "sandwich" story ("B"), a large

crowd is gathering around Jesus and is pressing in on many sides. From this large crowd, our woman enters the scene by touching the hem of Jesus's cloak. She is healed. Power leaves Jesus. We'll return to this. Then we return to the original story ("A2") as Jesus is swept away to the home of Jairus and is told that his daughter has died. But, Jesus tells the girl, "Talitha cum," which is Aramaic for "Little girl, get up!" Immediately, the girl gets up and walks around.

There are some lovely things that weave these stories together and enhance the sandwiched story of our study. There are so many delightful connections between the two stories. Some are pointed out by biblical scholar Beverly Zink-Sawyer, who observes:

> Both victims of illness are female and ritually unclean, one as a result of death and one as a result of hemorrhage; both represent the significance of the number twelve in Jewish tradition (the twelve years of hemorrhage and the twelve-year-old girl); and both are regarded as "daughters" (the little girl being Jairus's daughter and the woman who is addressed by Jesus as "Daughter"). An act of touch restores both women to new life even as those surrounding them lack understanding.[1]

Mural of the bleeding woman touching the hem of Jesus's garment, Encounter Chapel, Duc in Altum, Magdala, Israel

[1] Beverly Zink-Sawyer, "Homiletical Perspective" in *Feasting on the Word: Preaching the Revised Common Lectionary*, Vol. 3, Year B, David Lyon Bartlett and Barbara Brown Taylor, eds., (Louisville: Westminster John Knox Press, 2009), 191.

Immediately, we can notice the biblical significance with the number 12 that has connections all over the place. For these women, 12 years of bleeding and 12 years of age. We also can see that these two feminine characters are unnamed by society, but then beautifully placed by Jesus when he refers to both of them as "daughter." A sweet, intimate naming that is so needed by both of these women. Another intimate moment is the act of touch seen in both stories.

Jesus meets her in this space—or rather, is met by her—and does the opposite of what is expected.

Women know what it's like to bleed. Men do too, of course, but women have a cleansing of sorts that happens every month. We lose a part of our body every month and it is a painful, centering, mindful, difficult time. Even from biblical times, the idea of having blood outside of the body has been considered unclean or dirty. I find it unfortunate that the blood that is shed by women routinely for the sake of giving life has been shamed throughout history, while the blood shed by men in battle—in the act of taking life—is honored. Women, simply by having a body that works, were considered unclean and cast out routinely. This unnamed woman, whose story the text brings to light, not only suffered from continuous bleeding for many years, but also that dirty, unclean feeling resulting from being stigmatized and isolated. Hers was a continual existence of pain and being cast out. Jesus meets her in this space—or, rather, is met by her—and does the opposite of what is expected. Instead of being repulsed or disgusted by her, he responds with peace. He responds with acceptance and grace. He seems to respond with understanding. He calls her daughter. He accepts her. He offers her peace and heals her.

#SheIsCalled and We Are Called

This bleeding woman's story interacts with all of our stories because we, like her, have been in need of healing at some point or another. We have been outcasts or have felt abandoned by our communities or our friends. We have been in need of a merciful touch by God and by the body of Christ incarnate in our sisters and brothers here with us. Think of a time when you felt like you were at your end. Think of that space and ask God to show you where Jesus was in that space. What was he like? What did he refer to you as?

These stories are not telling us that we will always be healed, but rather, what it looks like to reach out to Jesus in times of pain and heartache, isolation and loneliness, in order to receive the gift of truth: you are beloved and known intimately by your creator.

One personal affirmation in this biblical story is that, beyond even physical healing, acceptance, intimacy, and touch can make us whole and give us peace. We are, in fact, shaped and made human *in relationship* to other persons. Our relationships—in the church, in friendships, and in marriage—are not just something extra added on to life for distraction and entertainment, as if we would be complete human beings in individual isolation. Relationship, "touch" if you will, makes us human and whole.[2]

Conclusion

Know that you are beloved and known by God. Healing does not always look exactly like what we are hoping for, but sometimes healing looks like acceptance, belonging, and connection. Sometimes healing looks like not letting fear have a hold in your life. Love looks like a touch from a friend or loved one in a moment of shame, hopelessness, or deep pain to draw us out and remind us that we are loved and called children of God.

Reach out and touch the robe of Jesus today and ask for the

---

[2] Michael L. Lindvall, "Pastoral Perspective," in Bartlett and Taylor, eds., *Feasting on the Word*, 192.

reminder, the grace, and the knowing that comes from him. Let Christ find you wherever you are and meet you there—at your lowest lows and your highest heights. Remember that you too are the hands of Christ and have the ability to offer healing to those who are suffering. Ask for wisdom and pray for strength and courage this day.

💬 Discussion Questions

1. Does healing always involve physical restoration? Is there a difference between being healed and being cured?
2. Share a story of healing from your own life.
3. What do you resonate with most from this story, and what is most challenging to you?
4. What surprised you in this Bible study session?
5. What do you hear the Spirit saying to you/your family/your church/your community?

Rev. Alisha Riepma *is an Albany Synod Fellow currently serving Prattsville Reformed Church and the Jay Gould Memorial Reformed Church in the Catskill Mountains of New York. She is passionate about youth, equity, and justice, looking to the church to lead the way in a revolutionary way of being in the world today. She is a member of the Women's Transformation and Leadership Guiding Coalition.*

Notes

grief

TRAUMA

SILENCE

Redemption

Turning Tragedy into Triumph

One Woman's Vigil for Justice

By Rev. Terry Ann Smith, Ph.D., and Rev. Micah L. McCreary, Ph.D.

🕯 Prayer

Dear Lord, open our eyes to the life and story of Rizpah. Move out of the way the ideologies, ideas, and identities that prevent her story from coming to life during this Bible study. Show us how the power of silence can serve as a countercultural protest in our efforts to build your church. Empower this story and each student to understand this woman's story as a gift to our learning, growing, and challenging lives of faith. In Christ's name we pray! Amen.

🔑 Key Scripture

2 Samuel 21:1-14
"Then Rizpah the daughter of Aiah took sackcloth, and spread it on a rock for herself, from the beginning of harvest until rain fell on them from the heavens; she did not allow the birds of the air to come on the bodies by day, or the wild animals by night."
—2 Samuel 21:10

★ Main Point

Grief and trauma are strange traveling companions, particularly when the circumstances surrounding tragic events are beyond our control. As people of faith, our response in these difficult moments can be life-defeating or life-affirming. This Bible study examines one woman's response to tragedy. In 2 Samuel 21, we meet Rizpah, a mother grieving over the untimely deaths of her two sons. Through her silence, we are confronted with the uncomfortable realities that accompany inequitable distributions of power. Yet, it is her silence, as a powerful testimony of a mother's pain, love, and courage, that reassures us to be steadfast in our faith since God can turn our most tragic moments into our greatest triumphs.

♟ Introduction to Rizpah

In 2 Samuel 21:1-14, a three-year famine has caused King David to "inquire of the LORD" of its cause. The problem, according to the LORD, is due to King Saul (now deceased) and his house who "put the Gibeonites to death" (21:1). King David approaches the Gibeonites and asks what he can do for the Gibeonites to "bless the heritage of the LORD," by which he means to bless David, the land, and the people of Judah (21:3). The Gibeonites (who are not Israelites, according to 21:2) exploit the Levitical law of retributive justice (Leviticus 24:17-22) against Saul (21:5), and since Saul is no longer living, against his descendants. It is under this backdrop of revenge and retribution that Rizpah enters our purview. She is the widow of the dethroned and deceased Saul, and while mentioned twice overall in biblical narrative (2 Samuel 3, 21), she makes a physical appearance only once, in the present story. In 2 Samuel 3, she is the subject of Ishbosheth's accusation against Abner of sexual assault. Although it is unclear whether Abner rapes Rizpah, the text gives voice to the vulnerability and tenuousness of her situation as a lower wife of a dead king. In the present text, this widow's woes are intensified as her sons, together with five of Saul's grandsons, are ritually slaughtered in a shocking episode that is part human sacrifice and part sanctioned execution.

📗 Digging Deeper

The Gibeonites' execution of the seven sons of Saul is violent in its presentation and violent in its proclamation. Under the guise of reconciliation and retributive justice, one is astonished by the callous abuse of power and the manipulation of religious symbols that pejoratively reflect on David, the Gibeonites, and God. Yet, the violent nature of the narrative is interrupted by the actions of a mother in mourning. Rizpah does for her sons in death what she cannot do for them in life; that is, protect them from predators. Here, we witness a grieving mother taking up a silent vigil over their corpses left exposed on a hill (21:9, 10). She could not stop David from taking her sons, could not stop the Gibeonites from killing them. So, she does what she can. The text says that she stands guard "from the beginning of the harvest till the rain poured down from the heavens on the bodies, she did not let the birds of the air touch them by day or the wild animals by night" (21:10). Wil Gafney paints a vivid portrait of Rizpah's vigil:

> Rizpah bat Aiah watches the corpses of her sons stiffen, soften, swell, and sink into the stench of decay … fights with winged, clawed, and toothed scavengers night and day. She is there from the spring harvest until the fall rains, as many as six months from Nissan (March/April) to Tishrei (September/October), sleeping, eating, toileting, protecting, and bearing witness.[1]

Rizpah's silent vigil over the dead bodies of these sons is evidence of her grief and becomes the visible bodily response to the traumatic and tragic conditions attending their deaths and her powerlessness to protect them from violence. She is subordinate to the coercive and abusive control that the king exerts over the lives and bodies of his subjects. For her, the matter of justice remains elusive, not simply because traumatic experiences harbor wounds that won't go

---

[1]   Wil Gafney, *Womanist Midrash: A Reintroduction to the Women of the Torah and the Throne* (Louisville: Westminster John Knox Press, 2017), 200–201.

away but also because she is unable to confront the king directly and exact the justice that the deaths of her sons demanded.

And yet, despite appearances of powerlessness, her truth (and the justice it demands) shames the most powerful person of her day, King David, to act on behalf of the dead (21:11). In a narrative twist of fate, her vigil becomes both a lament and remembrance that draws public attention and recourse. Gafney summarizes the point well: "lynching Rizpah's and Merab's sons did not heal the land or the people. Doing right by the multiply wronged woman did," as the text states, is only accomplished after David retrieves and buries the remains of the slain. It is only then that "God heeded supplications for the land" (2 Sam 21:14).[2] These words serve as the final commentary on this tragic tale in which God not only remains with us in the midst of our tragic and traumatic moments but allows us to triumph when we persevere.

> *God not only remains with us in the midst of our tragic and traumatic moments but allows us to triumph when we persevere.*

#SheIsCalled and We Are Called

On a hot summer night in August of 1955, 14-year-old African American Emmett Till was removed from his relatives' home in Mississippi by two white men. He was taken to a barn, stripped naked, pistol-whipped, shot in the head, and his lifeless body dumped in the Tallahatchie River. Emmett Till's body was returned to his mother in Chicago and upon witnessing the extent of the brutality enacted on the bloated unrecognizable corpse of her son, she refused attempts to bury him quietly. Insisting on an open casket ceremony, she said, "I wanted

---

2   Gafney, *Womanist Midrash*, 201.

the world to see what they did to my baby."[3] The disfigured body of Emmett Till on display to the entire world would shame a nation and usher in the Civil Rights Movement. In a modern context, Rizpah's silent vigil resonates with the cry for justice by countless mothers like Mamie Till-Mobley who have watched their children sacrificed to state-sanctioned brutality and the political and socio-economic exigencies of our society (Eric Garner, Trayvon Martin, Michael Brown, Kadi Diallo, and others). Jonathan Magonet suggests that Rizpah's actions represent "every mother who sees her sons killed before their time for reasons of state, be they in time of peace or in war. All that remains is for her to preserve the dignity of their memory and live on to bear witness and call to account the rulers of the world."[4] As these mothers bear witness to the memory of their loved ones, we are called to bear witness by "being with" them as they struggle with the pain of loss and the "de-centering" experiences that will forever change the world as they know it. In essence, we are called to abide with the traumatized in the most uncomfortable of spaces, providing the ministry of presence where there are no right answers and there are no simple fixes. This is not only the work of the shepherd or the work of pastoral care; but it is the work of the church and those who have been called to Christian service. When viewed from this perspective, it becomes not just one woman's triumph, but a triumph for us all. In the words of Christ, "when you have done this for the least of these, you have done it for me" (Matt. 25:40).

Conclusion

Rizpah's act could be understood as one that results in a small token of restorative justice. Some Christian theologians read Rizpah's vigil as a manifestation of the gift of powerlessness, sprinkled with the grace of surrender. This understanding makes it possible to view her vigil as an act of resistance where restoration is a feasible outcome.

---

[3] By multiple sources, this line is attributed to Emmett Till's mother.

[4] Jonathan Magonet, *Bible Lives* (London: SCM, 1992), 11.

In other words, she triumphs in the end. Yet, in this narrative, it is important that we ask who and what is being restored. Yes, Rizpah's vigil is powerful, but it is not redemptive. While she may have the satisfaction and closure of seeing her and Merab's sons buried, her grief and the trauma of their deaths remain an open wound. Thus, Rizpah's vigil must not be interpreted solely as an act of a peaceful warrior who operates with a heart of peace and a spirit of war. She must not be classified or categorized as a nonviolent resister to the evil of the situation. Her story is a wake-up call for those in theological education and the church to engage in the redemptive work that addresses the realities of traumatic suffering and help persons give meaning to their traumatic experiences. Current day Rizpahs can be ministered to in the shadow of the cross. Here, we offer that traumatized persons do not need church or biblical platitudes; they need a healing discourse that allows them to bear witness to their experience. If trauma is the "storm that does not go away," as Shelly Rambo suggests, then the church must be prepared to serve as lifeboats of redemption rooted in the Spirit and love of Christ.[5]

💬 Discussion Questions

1. How can silence become a mechanism to promote healing?
2. Discuss the significance of "being with" or "abiding with" a person during moments of tragedy.
3. What image of God is depicted in this story? Does this portrait of God make you comfortable or uncomfortable? Why?
4. How do you respond to the statement that "Rizpah's vigil is powerful, but not redemptive"?
5. What surprised you in this Bible study session?
6. What do you hear the Spirit saying to you/your family/your church/your community?

---

[5] Shelly Rambo, *Spirit and Trauma: A Theology of Remaining* (Westminster John Knox Press, 2010), 2.

Rev. Terry Ann Smith, Ph.D., *is the associate dean of Institutional Assessment and associate professor of Biblical Studies at New Brunswick Theological Seminary in New Brunswick, New Jersey. Her research interests and publications focus on inspections of the Hebrew Bible that expose normalized inequitable distributions of power and privilege as these intersect categories of ethnicity, class, and gender. As an ordained minister, she is particularly interested in contextualized socio-political readings of biblical texts that foster conversations within the church that address the theological, practical, and ethical applications of the Bible.*

Rev. Micah L. McCreary, Ph.D., *is president of New Brunswick Theological Seminary in New Brunswick, New Jersey, and a minister of Word and sacrament in the Reformed Church in America. Prior to coming to New Brunswick, Dr. McCreary served in the pastorate, psychological practice, and professorate at Virginia Commonwealth University in Richmond, Virginia. He studied engineering at the University of Michigan in Ann Arbor, Michigan, and theology at the Samuel DeWitt Proctor School of Theology at Virginia Union University in Richmond, Virginia. He received his M.S. and Ph.D. in counseling psychology from Virginia Commonwealth University in Richmond, Virginia.*

Appendix

General Resources on Women in the Bible

- Lockyer, Herbert. *All the Women of the Bible.* Zondervan: Grand Rapids, Michigan, 1988.
- Tucker, Ruth A. and Walter L. Liefield. *Daughters of the Church: Women and Ministry from New Testament Times to the Present.* Zondervan: Grand Rapids, Michigan, 1987.
- Tucker, Ruth A. *Dynamic Women of the Bible: What We Can Learn From Their Surprising Stories.* Baker Books: Grand Rapids, Michigan, 2014.

Resources on Difficult Texts on Women in the Bible

- Glahn, Sandra L., editor. *Vindicating the Vixens: Revisiting Sexualized, Vilified, and Marginalized Women of the Bible.* Kregel Academic: Grand Rapids, Michigan, 2017.
- Trible, Phyllis. *Texts of Terror: Literary-Feminist Readings of Biblical Narratives.* Fortress Press: Minneapolis, Minnesota, 1984.

Resources for Further Study

Session 1: Phoebe: Deacon and Benefactor
by Dr. Rob Dixon

- Video about Phoebe from Dr. Paula Gooder: https://www.youtube.com/watch?v=7m9-HWICvrg&t=30s
- Gooder, Paula. *Phoebe: A Story.* InterVarsity Press Academic: Downers Grove, Illinois, 2018.
- McKnight, Scot. *Junia Is Not Alone.* Ebook. https://www.amazon.com/Junia-Not-Alone-Scot-McKnight-ebook/dp/B006H4PFZ8/
- Mowczko, Margaret. "Paul and Women, in a Nutshell." Blog. October 6, 2014. https://margmowczko.com/paul-and-women-in-a-nutshell/

Session 2: The Samaritan Woman at the Well: Called To Be a Disciple and Evangelist
by Rev. Dustyn Elizabeth Keepers

- Keepers, Dustyn Elizabeth, ed. *Before the Face of God: Essays in Honor of Tom Boogaart.* Reformed Church Press: Grand Rapids, Michigan, 2019.
- Cohick, Lynn. *Women in the World of the Earliest Christians: Illuminating Ancient Ways of Life.* Baker Academic: Ada, Michigan, 2009.

Session 3: A Time to Embrace and A Time to Refrain from Embracing!
by Rev. Denise L. Posie

- Posie, Denise L. *Consider a Greater Purpose: Esther, Vashti and the Courageous Women who Followed.* Fortitude Graphic Design & Printing: Kalamazoo, Michigan: 2015.
- Includes work on both Deborah and Esther: *Leading Ladies: Transformative Biblical Images for Women's Leadership* by Jeanne Porter (Innisfree Press: Philadelphia, Pennsylvania, 2000).
- Haddad, Mimi. "Esther, the Earliest Silence Breaker." Blog. CBE International. March 18, 2019. https://www.cbeinternational.org/

resource/article/mutuality-blog-magazine/esther-earliest-silence-breaker

Session 4: Elizabeth and Mary: Called to Encourage One Another
by Rev. Dustyn Elizabeth Keepers

- Story, J. Lyle. "The Discipleship of Women." Priscilla Papers. CBE International. January 30, 2007. https://www.cbeinternational.org/resource/article/priscilla-papers-academic-journal/discipleship-women
- Cohick, Lynn. *Women in the World of the Earliest Christians: Illuminating Ancient Ways of Life.* Baker Academic: Ada, Michigan, 2009.
- Carman, Amy Smith. "Ave Maria: Old Testament Allusions in the Magnificat." Priscilla Papers. CBE International. April 29, 2017. https://www.cbeinternational.org/resource/article/priscilla-papers-academic-journal/ave-maria-old-testament-allusions-magnificat

Session 5: Priscilla and Aquila: The First Century Church's Dynamic Duo
by Rev. Tim Breen

- Mowczko, Margaret. "At Home with Priscilla and Aquila." Blog. November 11, 2015. https://margmowczko.com/at-home-with-priscilla-and-aquila/
- Priscilla and Aquila are large players in Phoebe's story: *Phoebe: A Story* by Paula Gooder. InterVarsity Press Academic: Downers Grove, Illinois, 2018.
- Witherington III, Ben. *Priscilla: The Life of an Early Christian.* InterVarsity Press Academic: Downers Grove, Illinois, 2019.
- Armas, Kat. "Priscilla and Aquila Model Marriage 'More Accurately.'" Blog. January 28, 2018. https://www.cbeinternational.org/resource/article/mutuality-blog-magazine/priscilla-and-aquila-model-marriage-more-accurately

Session 6: Zipporah: Called to Remind Us Who We Are
by Rev. Dr. Denise Kingdom Grier

- Gafney, Wilda. "A Womanist Midrash on Zipporah." Essay in *I Found God in Me: A Womanist Biblical Hermeneutics Reader.* Smith, Mitzi J., ed. Cascade Books: Eugene, Oregon, 2015.
- Mowczko, Margaret. "6 Women Who Protected and Rescued Moses." Blog. August 24, 2011. https://margmowczko.com/the-women-who-protected-moses/

Session 7: Deborah: Embracing the Call of God
by Pastor Pam Otten

- Japinga, Lynn. *Preaching the Women of the Old Testament: Who They Were and Why They Matter.* Westminster John Knox Press: Louisville, Kentucky, 2017.
- Mowczko, Margaret. "Deborah, and the 'No Available Men' Argument." Blog. June 28, 2012. https://margmowczko.com/deborah-and-the-no-available-men-argument/
- Mowczko, Margaret. "What's in a Name? Deborah, Woman of Lappidoth." Blog. November 28, 2015. https://margmowczko.com/deborah-woman-of-lappidoth/
- A resource on discernment and listening for God's voice. Virkler, Mark & Patti. *4 Keys to Hearing God's Voice.* Shippensburg, Pennsylvania: Destiny Image, 2010. https://www.amazon.com/4-Keys-Hearing-Gods-Voice/dp/0768432480/

Session 8: "Daughter, your faith has made you well."
by Rev. Alisha Riepma

- A novel with a different take on a woman's sacred journey: *The Red Tent - 20th Anniversary Edition* by Anita Diamant. (Picador: London, 2007.)
- Blanco, Lauren Gross. "Jesus Sees You: Endometriosis, the Bleeding Woman, and Me." Blog. March 24, 2020. https://www.cbeinternational.org/resource/article/mutuality-blog-magazine/jesus-sees-you-endometriosis-bleeding-woman-and-me
- Stiles, Eliza. "'Precious Food of True Life': Christ Our Mother,

Female Embodiment, and the Eucharist in Julian of Norwich's Revelations of Divine Love." Priscilla Papers. CBE International. https://www.cbeinternational.org/resource/article/priscilla-papers-academic-journal/precious-food-true-life-christ-our-mother-female

Session 9: Turning Tragedy into Triumph: One Woman's Vigil for Justice
by Rev. Terry Ann Smith, Ph.D., and Rev. Micah L. McCreary, Ph.D.

- On Emmett Till - "Emmett Till is Murdered," https://www.history.com/this-day-in-history/the-death-of-emmett-till
- Rambo, Shelly. *Spirit and Trauma: A Theology of Remaining.* Westminster John Knox Press: Louisville, Kentucky, 2010.
- Beaumont, Susan. *How to Lead When You Don't Know Where You Are Going: Leading in a Liminal Season.* Rowman & Littlefield Publishers: Lanham, Maryland, 2019.
- Crowder, Stephanie Buckhanon. *When Momma Speaks: The Bible and Motherhood from a Womanist Perspective.* Westminster John Knox Press: Louisville, Kentucky, 2016.
- tsmith@nbts.edu; mmccreary@nbts.edu

Notes

For more information on She is Called resources, contact:
Women's Transformation and Leadership

Email: women@rca.org
Website: www.rca.org/women
Facebook: She is Called, www.facebook.com/
womenstransformationandleadership